SHORT CIR____

WAL__

IN

CHARNWOOD

FOREST

by

JOHN N. MERRILL

Maps and photographs by John N. Merrill

TRAIL CREST PUBLICATIONS Ltd.,
- "from footprint to finished book."

1994

View south along
the Sandia Crest Trail,
9,000 feet up in New Mexico, USA.

TRAIL CREST PUBLICATIONS Ltd.,
Milne House,
Speedwell Mill,
Miller's Green,
Wirksworth,
Derbyshire
DE4 4BL

FAX (01629) 826354
(01629) 826354

Edited, typeset, designed, paged, printed, marketed and distributed by John N. Merrill.

© Text, & photographs - John N. Merrill 1994.
© Maps - John N. Merrill 1994.

First Published - July 1992
Reprinted April 1993.
This edition September 1994

Printed on100% recycled paper.

ISBN 0 907496 92 X
Please note - The maps in this guide are purely illustrative. You are encouraged to use the appropriate 1:25,000 O.S. map.

U.S.A.
office -
P.O. Box 124,
Santa Rosa,
New Mexico
88435
U.S.A.

Meticulous research has been undertaken to ensure that this publication is highly accurate at the time of going to press. The publishers, however, cannot be held responsible for alterations, errors or omissions, but they would welcome notification of such for future editions.

Typeset in - Times - bold, italic and plain 9pt and 18pt.

Printed and designed by - Footprint Press Ltd./John N. Merrill at Milne House, Speedwell Mill, Miller's Green, Wirksworth, Derbyshire. DE4 4BL.
Cover sketch - "Beacon Hill" by John Creber
© Suncrest Ventures Ltd. 1994.

An all British product.

CONTENTS

ABOUT JOHN N. MERRILL

Born in the flatlands of Bedfordshire he soon moved to Sheffield and discovered the joy of the countryside in the Peak District, where he lives. A keen walker who travels the world exploring mountains and trails. Over the last twenty years he has walked more than 150,000 miles - including the first walk around the entire coastline of Britain, 7,000 miles - and worn out over eighty pairs of boots. He has written more than 130 walk guides to areas in Britain and abroad, and created numerous challenge walks which have been used to raise more than £500,000 for charity. New Mexico, USA is his second home.

INTRODUCTION

I first began walking in the area in 1960's, writing walks for a National camping magazine. I fell in love with the area - Bradgate Park, Grace Dieu Priory, Mount St. Bernard Abbey and Ulverscroft Priory. I wandered around them all and scaled the rocky heights. I never thought that It would be more than twenty years before I returned to fully explore the area and revisit some of my favourite haunts.

In this book I have endeavoured to explore all the excellent walking there is to be found in the Charnwood Forest area of Leicester - the "hilly country". But I have broadened the area to take in Ashby de la Zouch and its canal on the western side. Just to level it off I have included a canal walk on the eastern side. The most southern walk takes in the Ashby Canal and the Battle of Bosworth site - a very rewarding and interesting walk.

All the walks have their own charm and character. The one from Ratby to Thornton Reservoir is outstanding ; with the reservoir located in a most attractive setting. Bradgate Park is quite beautiful with the door and ruined hall; the ascent to Bardon Hill and the Warren Hills makes you realise that Leicestershire is not flat! The encirclement of Beacon Hill and its views to Loughborough and Nottinghamshire is a delightful circuit. So too is the one round Mount St. Bernard Abbey and Blackbrook Reservoir. The ruins of Ulverscroft Priory and Grace Dieu Priory are worth walking round to see. The most northern walk is a short one to the summit of Breedon on the Hill; again the view is extensive but the village is worth exploring as well as the church on the top of the hill.

Here then are fifteen walks in the Charnwood Forest area of Leicester - some short, some long - taking you into woodland, parkland, past ruined monastic buildings, over rocky hills and along peaceful secluded canals. I hope you enjoy the walks, like I have, and come to admire the scenic countryside of Charnwood Forest.

Happy walking!
John N. Merrill
1994

ABOUT THE WALKS

Whilst every care is taken detailing and describing the walk in this book, it should be borne in mind that the countryside changes by the seasons and the work of man. I have described the walk to the best of my ability, detailing what I have found on the walk in the way of stiles and signs. Obviously with the passage of time stiles become broken or replaced by a ladder stile or even a small gate. Signs too have a habit of being broken or pushed over. All the route follow rights of way and only on rare occasions will you have to overcome obstacles in its path, such as a barbed wire fence or electric fence. On rare occasions rights of way are rerouted and these ammendments are included in the next edition.

The seasons bring occasional problems whilst out walking which should also be borne in mind. In the height of summer paths become overgrown and you will have to fight your way through in a few places. In low lying areas the fields are often full of crops, and although the pathline goes straight across it may be more practical to walk round the field edge to get to the next stile or gate. In summer the ground is generally dry but in autumn and winter, especially because of our climate, the surface can be decidedly wet and slippery; sometimes even gluttonous mud!

These comments are part of countryside walking which help to make your walk more interesting or briefly frustrating. Standing in a farmyard up to your ankles in mud might not be funny at the time but upon reflection was one of the highlights of the walk!

The mileage for each walk is based on three calculations -

1. pedometer reading.
2. the route map measured on the map.
3. the time I took for the walk.

I believe the figure stated for each walk to be very accurate but we all walk differently and not always in a straight line! The time allowed for each walk is on the generous side and does not include pub stops etc. The figure is based on the fact that on average a person walks 2 1/2 miles an hours but less in hilly terrain.

Deer in Bradgate Park.

Bradgate ruins - walk 9.

BREEDON ON THE HILL - 2 MILES

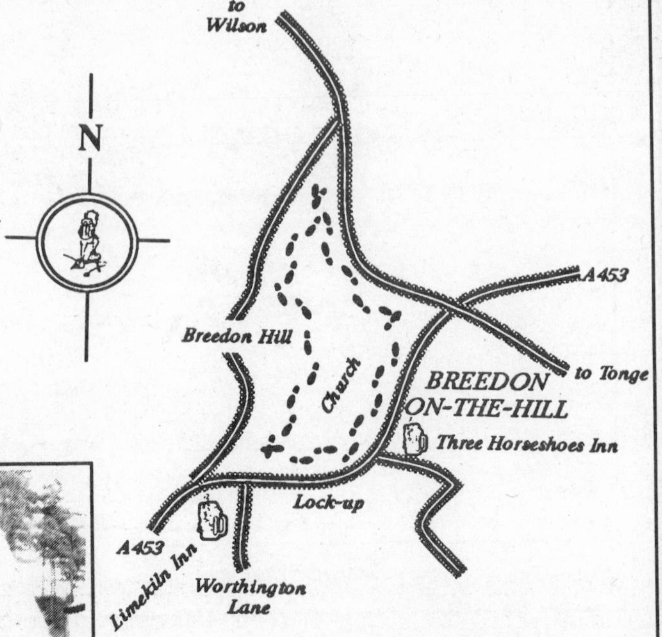
to
Wilson
N
A453
Breedon Hill
Church
BREEDON
ON-THE-HILL
to Tonge
Three Horseshoes Inn
Lock-up
A453
Limekiln Inn
Worthington
Lane

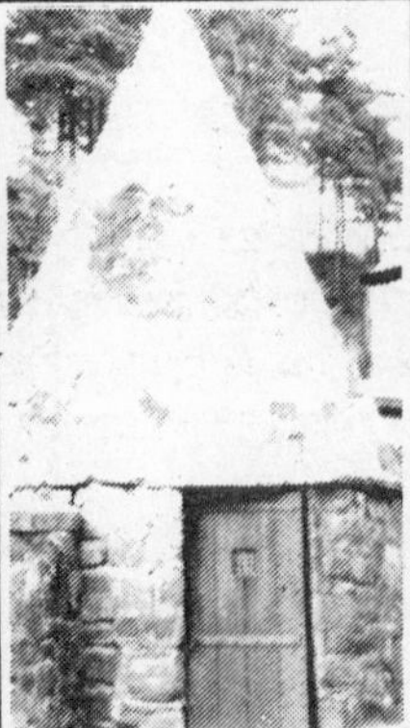

Lock-up

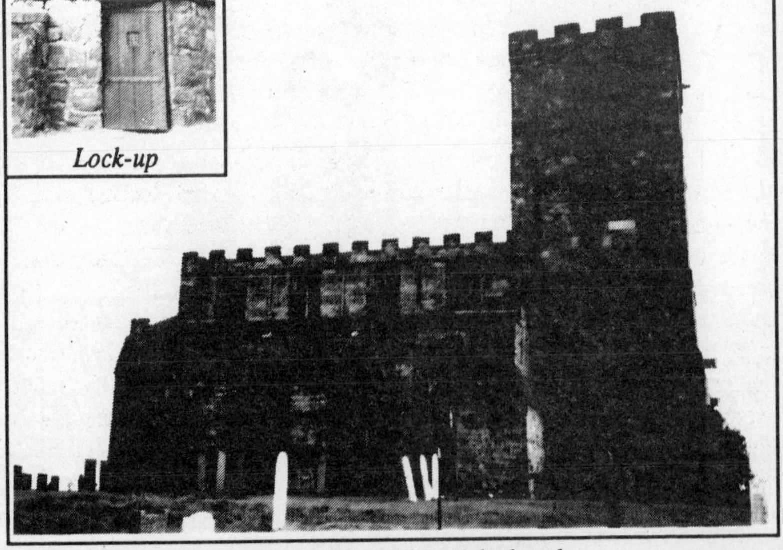

Breedon on the Hill Parish church.

BREEDON ON THE HILL
- 2 MILES
- allow 1 hour.

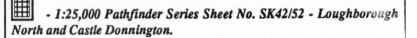 *- Breedon on the Hill - Breedon Hill - Parish Church - Breedon on the Hill.*

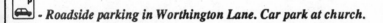 *- 1:25,000 Pathfinder Series Sheet No. SK42/52 - Loughborough North and Castle Donnington.*

- Roadside parking in Worthington Lane. Car park at church.

- Lime Kiln Inn and Three Horseshoes Inn, Breedon on the Hill.

ABOUT THE WALK - A very short one but the ascent to the church on the top of the hill is outstanding. The views are extensive to the East Midlands Airport, motor racing circuit and over Derbyshire. But the crux of the walk is the church. Dating back to Saxon times, the exterior has Norman workmanship and inside is full of Saxon workmanship - carvings and friezes - an array unequalled. At the start and end of the walk you see the village lock-up, used for misbehaving locals in the 19th century. The walk starts from Worthington road, as I always feel the view and splendour of the hill must be earnt!

WALKING INSTRUCTIONS - From Worthington Road turn right along the Main Street (A453), passing the road The Delph and lock up on your left - it is down there you will return. Pass the Three Horseshoes Inn and 1/4 mile later just before the road junction to Tonge, turn left, walking past the house Deep Well on your right. It is footpath signed and well trodden. The path keeps to the edge of the quarry, through woodland and just above the road to Wilson. After 1/2 mile follow the path round to your left, with views of the hill and church and on your right a golf course. Continue on the path and eventually ascend to road near the top of Breedon Hill. Continue to the church. Follow the road on the left of the church and gain a footpath/track and begin descending gently down towards the village. Gaining a road turn left along it, keeping left at the next junction, and walk down The Delph back to the Main Street and Lock up.

ASHBY DE LA ZOUCH
- 5 MILES

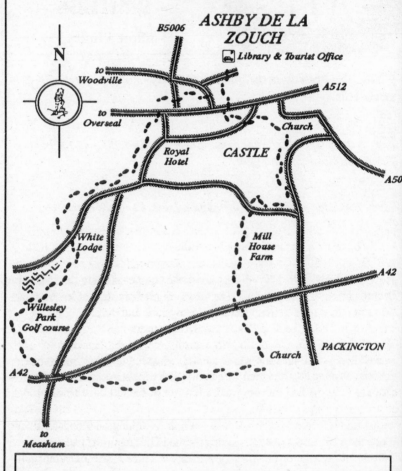

ASHBY DE LA ZOUCH

Library & Tourist Office

B5006

to Woodville

to Overseal

A512

A50

Church

Royal Hotel

CASTLE

N

White Lodge

Mill House Farm

A42

Willesley Park Golf course

A42

Church

PACKINGTON

to Measham

Ashby de la Zouch Castle.

ASHBY DE LA ZOUCH
- 5 MILES

- allow 2 hours.

•• •• •• *- Ashby De La Zouch - Castle - Mill House Farm - A42 - Packington - A42 - Willesley Park - B5006 - Ashby De La Zouch.*

- 1:25,000 Pathfinder Series Sheet No. 873 (SK 21/31) - Ashby De La Zouch.

and start - Beside Library & Tourist Office - Grid Ref. SK 358168.

Several others around the town.

- Numerous in Ashby De La Zouch at the start or end of the walk.

ABOUT THE WALK - A pleasant walk around the countryside to the south of the town. En route you can explore the castle ruins and the village of Packington, just off the route. You return through Willesley Park and its golf course and can visit Willesley church close to the route.

WALKING INSTRUCTIONS - Return to the road from the car park, passing the library and Tourist Information Office on your left. Cross the road, as footpath signed to the town, and walk along Mill Lane Mews passing the shops to the main street and shops. Cross over to your left and walk through an alley and past a car park to the road - footpath signed for the castle. Turn left passing the entrance to castle on your right. At the top of the road where it turns sharp left, keep ahead and walk past St. Helen's church on your right. Gaining the road turn right and walk along a tarmaced path past the Manor School and the castle on your right. Reaching a road keep straight ahead along it, crossing a railway line and Windmill Hill. In little over 1/4 mile turn right along a road with the "Old Ashbeians R.F.C." on your left. In less than 1/4 mile where the road turns sharp right, turn left as footpath signed, and walk along the track towards Mill House Farm. Approaching the farm turn left, as path signed, to a stile. Bear right across the field to its righthand side and walk along the field boundary to a footbridge. Just after cross another and turn right to two footbridges. Ahead in the A42. Turn right and angle towards the road where there is a footbridge. Cross over and turn left then right and walk along a track to the righthand side of Packington village and a lane.

Walk along the lane to the church and turn right through a stile and walk along the edge of a football field to another stile. Over this follow a defined path across the field and once over the rise gain another stile. Ahead can be seen the A42; continue towards it and a stile. Cross the minor road and walk through the underpass and turn left to a stile and footpath sign. Enter Willersley Park with the golf course on your right. Enter woodland and keep to the righthand path. Cross a fairway, guided by yellow topped posts and reach a minor road. Turn right and in 100 yards turn right along a track on the right of South Lodge - on your right is the golf course. Continue along the track and soon pass a scout camp on your left and Willesley church. Follow the track round to your right then left with views of Willesley lake. In little over 1/2 mile from the lodge, turn left through a stile by a footpath sign. Descend the field and cross the end of the lake and reach the road beside White Lodge. Turn right and follow the road - Willesley Road. In 3/4 mile join the B5006 road and follow it back into Ashby De La Zouch, passing the Royal Hotel. Turn right in the main shopping area and retrace your steps back along Mill Lane Mews back to the car park.

ASHBY DE LA ZOUCH - The castle was a originally a Norman Manor house and was granted to the first Baron Hastings in 1461. The Hastings family have been associated with the castle for centuries. Mary Queen of Scots was imprisoned here in 1569 and 1586. During the Civil War much of the castle was demolished. Sir Walter Scott's book "Ivanhoe" is set nearby. St. Helen's church contains glass from the castle and a unique 13 grooved finger pillory.

Ruins of Grace Dieu Priory - see walk 3.

12

Ashby de la Zouch Canal - walks 14 & 15.

Milepost.

OSGATHORPE AND GRACE DIEU PRIORY - 5 MILES

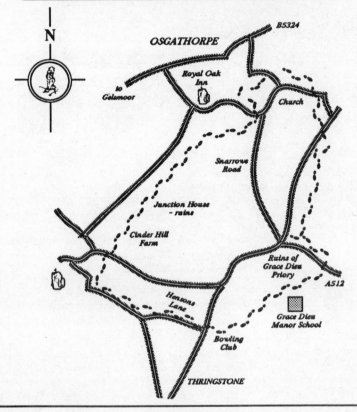

- from opposite page -

Reaching the main road cross over and walk along Hensons Lane and turn right along Main Street. Just around the first righthand corner is a stile on your right - if you continue down the lane you will come to the inn. The path Keeps to the edge of the field to a stile. Here turn left and descend to a stile and road. Cross over and walk along the farm road to Cinder Hill Farm. Bear left past the buildings to a gate. Through this turn right to a stile and keep the field boundary on your left- a fence. Continue to a stile and descend into a hollow and ascend the other side by the steps. You now walk along the top of a earthwork passing the ruins of Junction House. Continue on the path for a further 1/2 mile to a footpath sign and Snarrows Road. Turn left and left along Main Street. If you continue along here you will come to the Royal Oak Inn in Osgathorpe. But after a few yards turn right along a path beside the stream. At the end turn right into Church Lane where you began.

OSGATHORPE AND GRACE DIEU PRIORY
- 5 MILES
- allow 2 hours.

.. .. .. *- Osgathorpe - Abbey Ford Farm - Grace Dieu Priory - The Manor Farm - Grace Dieu Farm - Thringstone - Cinder Hill Farm - Junction House - Osgathorpe.*

- 1:25,000 Pathfinder Series Sheet No. 874 - (SK 41/51) - Loughborough (South).

- No official one. Roadside parking in Osgathorpe.

- None actually on the route, but just off it is the Royal Oak in Osgathorpe and one on the outskirts of Thringstone.

ABOUT THE WALK - Osgathorpe is a very attractive village and well worth exploring to see the church dedicated to St. Mary Blessed Virgin. You follow lanes to see the remains of Grace Dieu Priory before walking past Grace Dieu Manor School and woodland to Thringstone. From here you follow a path across the fields back to Osgathorpe. I first walked around here twenty years ago and was pleased to find it still an unspoilt gem, with skylarks in the air and lord and ladies growing in the hedgerows.

WALKING INSTRUCTIONS - From Church Lane on the north side of the church in Osgathorpe, walk eastwards along it past Harley House. Keep on the lane for more than 1/4 mile. After the second righthand bend look for a stile on your right. Turn right and walk beside the field hedge on your left to a stile, footpath sign, and road. Turn right along the road and follow it to the road junction 1/2 mile away; opposite in the field are the ruins of Grace Dieu Priory. Turn left along the road, walking along the wide verge, for little over 1/4 mile to the footpath sign and road to Grace Dieu Manor School. Walk along the drive and where it turns left to the school keep ahead to a stile. Keep to the righthand side of the field, passing The Manor Farm on your right and descending to a stile and woodland. Bear left through the woodland at first, then right then left and continue with the woodland on your left as the path becomes a track. Follow it round to your right passing Thringstone Bowling Club on your left.

- continued opposite -

MOUNT St. BERNARD ABBEY & BLACKBROOK RESERVOIR - 5 MILES

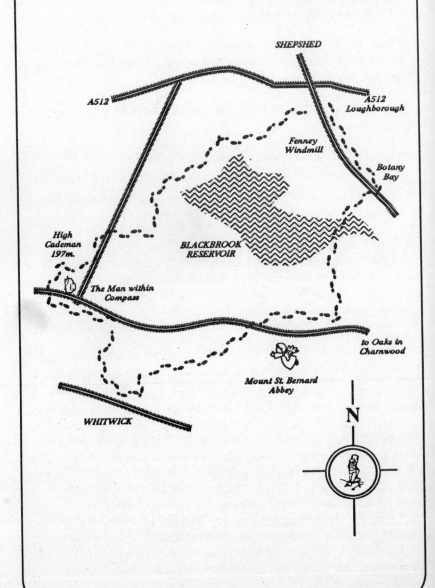

SHEPSHED

A512

A512
Loughborough

Fenney
Windmill

Botany
Bay

High
Cademan
197m.

BLACKBROOK
RESERVOIR

The Man within
Compass

to Oaks in
Charnwood

Mount St. Bernard
Abbey

WHITWICK

N

MOUNT ST. BERNARD ABBEY & BLACKBROOK RESERVOIR - 5 MILES - allow 2 hours.

Walk No 4

** .. ** - *A512 Blackbrook Hill - Blackbrook Reservoir - High Cademan - Whitwick - Ratchet Hill - Mount St. Bernard Abbey - Blackbrook Reservoir - Botany Bay - Fenney Windmill - Blackbrook Hill.*

- 1:25,000 Pathfinder Series Sheet No. 874 (SK41/51) Loughborough (South).

& start - No official car park, but roadside parking, just off the A512 road, at the crossroads near Fenney Windmill/Blackbrook Hill at Grid Ref. SK462183.

- The Man within Compass, below High Cademan.

ABOUT THE WALK - A particularly attractive walk through "mountain" country, past Blackbrook Reservoir and over rocky summits to Mount St. Bernard Abbey - you walk past the entrance gates and it is well worth the detour to visit this domain. You return past Blackbrook Reservoir again and descend a lane passing the magnificent Fenney Windmill back to the start.

WALKING INSTRUCTIONS - At the corner of the lane ascend the stile by the footpath sign - you can walk along the lane as this path simply cuts the corner off. Cross to a stile and the lane. Turn left along it following to woodland where it becomes a walled track and ascend to a gate on the edge of the woodland. To your left is Blackbrook Reservoir and its overflow. The right of way currently marked on the map has been diverted. From the gate turn left along the field edge to the next field. Here turn right walking close to the field boundary on your right for 1/4 mile before turning left along the field edge. In over 1/4 mile reach a gate by a footpath sign and a lane. Turn right along it to a road - Swannymote Road. Turn left and ascend for more than 1/4 mile with the rocky outcrop High Sharpley on your left. Pass woodland on your right and here you will find a stile and footpath sign. Turn right into the woodland around High Cademan, 197m. At first you keep close to the wall on your right in the woodland before bearing left to pass the rocky base of High

Cademan complete with triangulation pillar - it is worth the ascent for the view! Keep to the path to the right of the summit and in 100 yards or so turn left down a path that descends to a stile on the edge of woodland. Descend the field to a stile on your right and pass between the houses to a road. Turn left and in a few strides is the rather aptly named ' inn - "The Man Within Compass".

Continue along the road a short distance to just past the road junction with Swannymote Road and turn right along a track. In 200 yards just past a cluster of trees turn right at the stile and footpath sign. The path diagonally crosses the field to your right to the righthand corner and onto a road and the Leicester Road in Whitwick; gained near a shop on your right. Turn left and in 100 yards or so turn left, as footpath signed and follow a track which goes around the perimeter of a large quarry; again not as detailed on the current map. The track soon bears right as you walk past woodland of Rachet Hill on your left. 1/2 mile from the Whitwick gain a track junction. Turn right and in a few yards left as the stile and cross the fields, guided by stile to the road near Mount St. Bernard Abbey. Walk along the road past the entrance to the abbey on your right before turning left, at the footpath sign, and descend the fields to Blackbrook Reservoir. Close to the reservoir you turn right to a stile and footpath sign, Here gain a track the turn left along over the reservoir and onto the road, 1/4 mile away at Botany Bay. Turn left and descend the road past Fenney Windmill to the start.

MOUNT St. BERNARD ABBEY - The abbey was opened in 1835 and is the first Catholic Abbey in this country following the reformation. The monks are of the Cistercian Order. The abbey is open to the public and well worth visiting.

Blackbrook Reservoir.

Fenney Windmill.

The Bull's Head Inn - highest pub in Leicestershire - 787 ft. Walk 7.

BEACON HILL, 248M. - 2 MILES

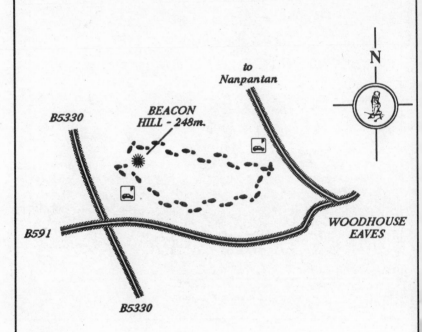

to
Nanpantan

BEACON
HILL - 248m.

B5330

B591

WOODHOUSE
EAVES

B5330

N

Rock escarpment - Beacon Hill.

BEACON HILL, 248m.
- 2 MILES
- allow 1 hour.

Beacon Hill - a complete encirclement of the hill from west to east in an anti-clockwise direction.

O.S. MAP - *1:25,000 Pathfinder Series Sheet No. 874 (SK 41/51) Loughborough (South).*

- The walk begins from the upper (western) car park, Grid Ref. SK509147.
Lower (eastern) car park at Grid Ref. SK523148.

- None; nearest in Woodhouse Eaves.

ABOUT THE WALK - Beacon Hill is a magnificent vantage point with a 360 degree view from its rocky summit. This short walk takes around the hill on a wide track; all the time you have views to Bradgate Park - Old John Tower; Loughborough and Charnwood Forest.

WALKING INSTRUCTIONS - Leave the car park (western one) by the wide path/track that goes through sparse woodland then beside it, as you descend gently, with the minor road (B591) on your right. After 1/2 mile the track swings away to your left to the lower car park. Gaining the car park turn left onto another well defined track, and now begin ascending through woodland and rhoderdendrons, at first, and in just under a mile reach the rocky outcrop of Beacon Hill on your left with triangulation pillar on top. Follow the track round to your left past the summit and descend back to the car park and start.

ULVERSCROFT PRIORY - 4 1/2 MILES

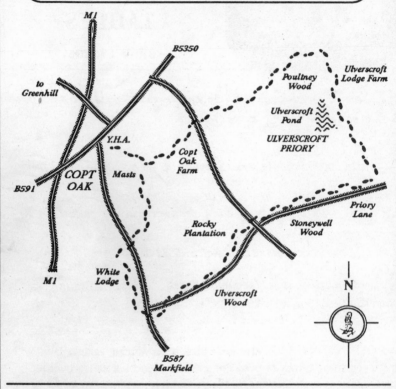

- from opposite page -

and a tall monument. Reach a stile and continue ahead with Ulverscroft Pond on your right. You soon gain a track which you walk around Ulverscroft Priory, and on to Priory Lane 1/4 mile away.

Turn right along the lane and ascend to a cross roads 1/2 mile away. Continue ahead, still on Priory Lane, past Rocky Plantation on your right and descend slightly before ascending to the B587 (Copt Hill) road. Here turn right and walk along the road for little over 1/4 mile. Just past White Hill Lodge on your left reach a stile and footpath sign on your right. Walk beside woodland to another stile where bear half left and descend to another stile and path sign - Whitecrofts Lane. Continue to another stile, ascending slightly to pass a large telecommunications tower on your left. Reach another stile and at the end of the next field another - the one you passed near the start of the walk, with Copt Oak Farm to your right. Turn left and retrace your steps back to St. Peter's church and Copt Oak.

ULVERSCROFT PRIORY
- 4 1/2 MILES

- allow 2 hours.

- Copt Oak - Poultney Wood - Ulverscroft Priory - Priory Lane - Rocky Plantation - B587 - Copt Oak.

 **- 1:25,000 Pathfinder Series Sheet No. 874 (SK 41/51) - Loughborough (South).**

- No official one; limited road side parking.

YHA - Copt Oak.

- The Copt Oak.

ABOUT THE WALK - A really delightful walk over fields and through woodland to the impressive ruins of Ulverscroft Priory. More than a mile of country lane walking brings you to your final footpath across the fields to Copt Oak; here is a youth hostel and eating house/inn. A walk that I have been walking for over twenty years - since I was a toddler!

WALKING INSTRUCTIONS - From the road junction at Copt Oak of the B5350 and B587 road, walk along the B587 past the Youth Hostel and before the Copt Oak Inn, turn left up the drive to St. Peter's church. Keep to the left of the church, as guided by yellow topped posts, and walk around a field edge to your right. Ascend a stile and soon afterwards turn left keeping the field edge on your left, and reach another stile. Still keep the field boundary on your left and gain another stile. Here you will notice another on your right - this is your return route. Keep to the righthand side of the field with Copt Oak Farm on your right and gain a small lane beside a path sign. Cross to your left to a stile and path sign. The path keeps beside the field boundary on your right and after a stile curves to your right to the edge of Poultney. Here turn left keeping the wood on your right and descend to two fields using gates. After the second one enter the woodland and keep straight ahead to another gate. Back in a field bear right to another gate, then left along the field edge to sparse woodland and a footbridge; all the time you are on a well defined path. Keep to the edge of the woodland and field with Ulverscroft Lodge Farm to your left

- continued opposite -

BARDON HILL
& WARREN HILLS - 5 1/2 MILES

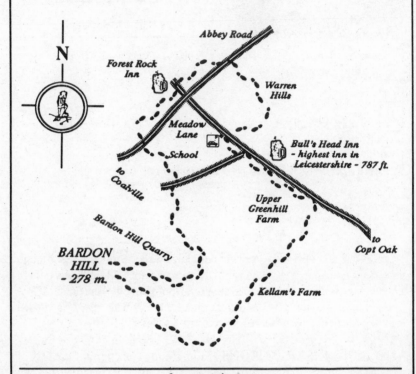

- from opposite page -

Retrace your steps back down the hill to near the ruined farm where there is a track. Turn left along this. Reaching a tarmaced road from the hill turn right and in 75 yards left along a track through the forest. The path keeps near to the righthand edge of the plantation and curves round to your left. After more than 1/2 mile bear right and leave the trees behind, continuing on a well defined path. Where it forks keeps straight ahead and gain a kissing gate. Continue past the houses of Greenhill to the road. Turn left then right along Stamford Drive. Turn right between houses 63 and 65, and follow the path along the edge of the estate with a large school playing field on your right. Little over 1/4 mile reach Meadow Lane and turn right and ascend to the cross roads beside the Forest Rock Inn. Keep straight ahead on Abbey Road. In 1/4 mile turn right at the stile and follow the path over the Warren Hills. In over 1/4 mile walk beside a wall on your left and in a further 1/4 mile reach a stile and bear right and descend to road and parking space where you began.

BARDON HILL & WARREN HILLS
- 5 1/2 MILES
- allow 2 hours.

⬛ ▄ ▀ *- Abbot's Oak - Upper Greenhill Farm - Kellam's Farm - Bardon Hill - Greenhill - Warren Hills - Abbot's Oak.*

🗺 *- 1:25,000 Pathfinder Series Sheet No. 874 - (SK 41/51) - Loughborough (South).*

🅿 *- No official one. Roadside parking beside footpath to Warren Hills, near Abbot's Oak at Grid Ref. 463145.*

🍺 *- Bull's Head, Abbot's Oak - the highest inn in Leicestershire at 787ft. Forest Rock Inn at cross roads before the Warren Hills.*

ABOUT THE WALK - From the lofty start of the walk you have the Warren Hills behind you and the view to Bardon Hill ahead. First you head for the wooded slopes of Bardon Hill before walking through woodland to Greenhill. Here you ascend to the impressive Warren Hills back to your start. The views are impressive throughout the walk.

WALKING INSTRUCTIONS - From the footpath sign beside the road for the Warren Hills, turn left along the road to Abbot's Oak and the Bull's Head Inn. Continue along the road to Copt Oak for 1/2 mile. Pass Upper Greenhill Farm on your right and turn right at the gate and footpath sign "To A50". Walk along the tarmaced surface and in more than 1/4 mile approach Kellam's Farm. Using the stile walk around the righthand side to a stile. Cross an avenue of trees to a gate and continue with the wall on your righthand side to another stile and wood on your right. Continue to the otherside of the wood and turn right at the stile, and ascend beside it to a stile. Cross the avenue of trees to your right to another stile and ascend to the right of a ruined farm, guided by yellow posts. Continue ahead and ascend the path through the pine trees to the summit of Bardon Hill and its trig point. The view over Bardon Hill Quarry may come as a shock!

- continued opposite -

SWITHLAND WOOD - 2 1/2 MILES

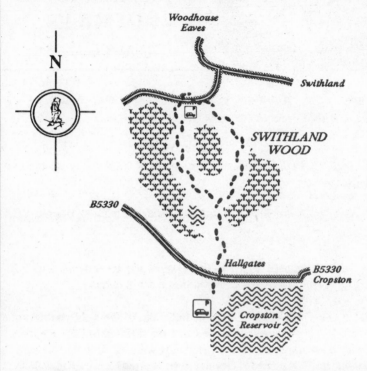

Quarry pond in Swithland Wood.

SWITHLAND WOOD
- 2 1/2 MILES
- allow 1 hour.

- Hallgates - Swithland Wood - Brand Hills - Swithland Wood - Hallgates.

O.S. MAP *- 1:25,000 Pathfinder Series Sheet No. 874 (SK 41/51) - Loughborough (South).*

- Hallgates - Bradgate Park, just off the B5330 road at Grid Ref. SK542114. Another at the northern end of Swithland Wood at Grid Ref. SK 538129.

- None on the walk. Nearest at Swithland and Woodhouse Eaves.

ABOUT THE WALK - A short circular walk around the medieval oak woodlands of Swithland Wood. Most of the time you are following a track.

WALKING INSTRUCTIONS - Return to the road - B5330 - from the car park and turn left. After a few yards turn right at the footpath sign - "Swithland". The path is defined and cross the field to your left aiming for the wood. In 1/4 mile cross a footbridge and enter the wood and gain a track on the right of a stone bridge. Turn right along the track and ignore all the side turnings. In 1/4 mile your pass the mounds of a quarry on your left - you will return to here on your way back. Continue ahead and in a short distance the track divides; keep to the lefthand branch. Continue through woodland and across an open space before entering woodland again and following the track round to your left to the road near Brand Hills. On your left is a water filled quarry, similar to the one you passed earlier although you have to climb up to see the water.

Turn left along the road to the car park. Walk through the car park and exit its top lefthand side along a good track. In 1/4 mile pass a mound on your left and 1/4 mile further bear left to your earlier track with the quarry mound on your right. Turn right and retrace your steps back to the bridge. Turn left and cross the footbridge and cross the field back to the road and car park at Hallgates.

BRADGATE PARK - 4 MILES

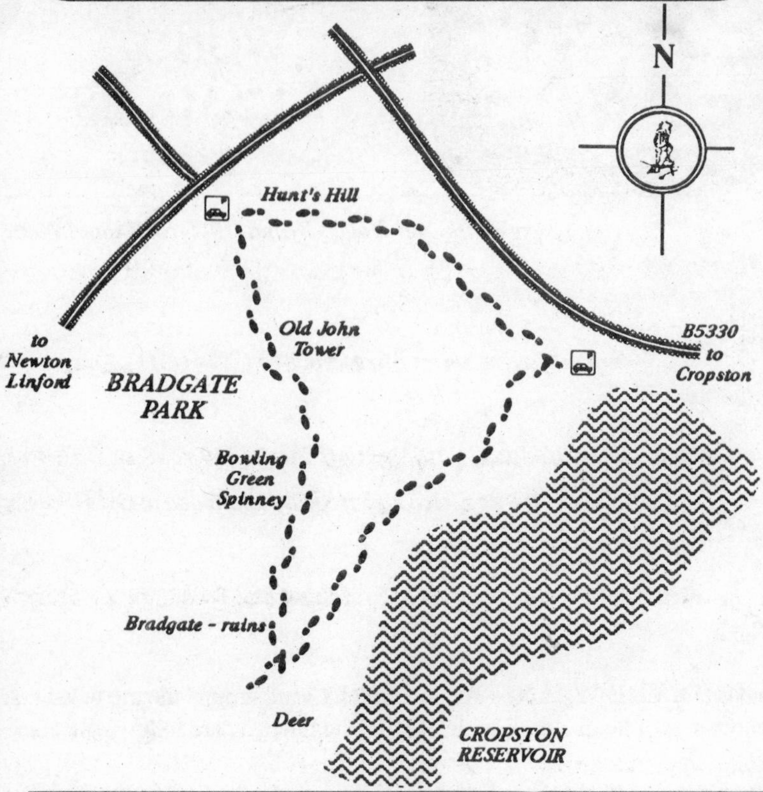

N
Hunt's Hill
Old John Tower
to Newton Linford
BRADGATE PARK
Bowling Green Spinney
Bradgate - ruins
Deer
B5330 to Cropston
CROPSTON RESERVOIR

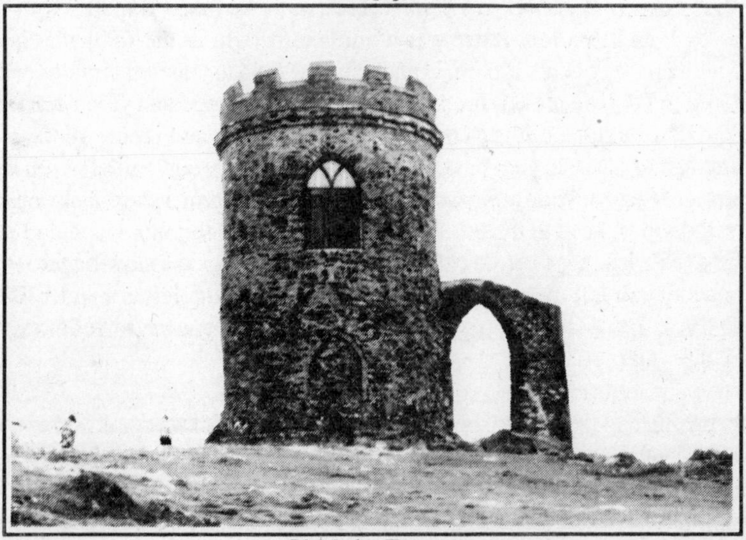

Old John Tower.

BRADGATE PARK - 4 MILES

- allow 1 1/2 hours.

Walk No 9

⬤⬤ ⬤⬤ ⬤⬤ *- Hunt's Hill Car Park - Old John Tower - Bradgate Park - Bowling Green Spinney - Bradgate House ruins - Cropston Reservoir - Hall Gates - Bradgate Park - Hunt's Hill.*

- 1:25,000 Pathfinder Series Sheet No. 874 (SK 41/51) Loughborough (South).

& start - North-west corner of Bradgate Park on the Newtown Linford road at Grid Ref. SK 523116. Another at Hallgates on the B5330 road at Grid Ref. SK543114.

- None on the walk; nearest at Newtown Linford and Woodhouse Eaves.

ABOUT THE WALK - Bradgate Park has always been the jewel of Charnwood Forest. A beautiful 850 acres of bracken, heath and woodland. A place where deer roam; a folly and the ruins of the birthplace of Lady Jane Grey, the eight day Queen of England. You encircle much of the park on a well walked track in an anti-clockwise direction.

WALKING INSTRUCTIONS - From the car park ascend the tarmaced path to the entrance to the park. Keep ahead and descend and ascend to the folly, built in 1786, - Old John Tower. A plaque here gives the distance to many sights over the surrounding area. Descend the other side, on a wide track/path, aiming for the lefthand side of the middle circular plantation - Bowling Green Spinney - 1/2 mile away. Keep to the path/track which keeps beside the Spinney on your immediate right and in 1/4 mile pass the ruins of Bradgate House on your left. Turn left to gain the tarmaced track passing the Queen Adelaide's Oak, where she pic-nicked in July 1842. Keep on the driveway, no doubt seeing many deer on your right, before views of Cropston Reservoir. Keep on the drive for 3/4 mile to the car park at Hallgates. Here turn left and walk through the car park and gain the path that curves to the boundary of the park. Begin ascending gently for more than a mile and reach your entrance point into the park on your right. Turn right and descend back to the car park.

GRAND UNION CANAL
- LEICESTER NAVIGATION
- 3 1/2 MILES

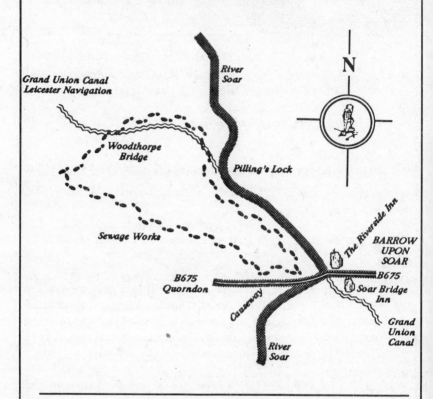

- from opposite page -

bear left to the far righthand corner of the field to a stile and footpath sign; just ahead is a sewage works. Turn right along the track past the works and in 1/4 mile leave it at the footpath sign. This final path across the fields to the B675 and Causeway is not used often. In theory you should go diagonally across the fields but not all the stiles are there. It maybe better to walk down the lane beside the sign and turn right and pick up the true pathline to the road, reached beside a pathsign. You can, of course, simply walk along the track to the road and turn left and walk along the Causeway back to the river Soar bridge.

GRAND UNION CANAL - One of the major canal systems linking the River Thames with Birmingham and the north. The Leicester section is 66 miles long and the part from Loughborough to Leicester was built in 1794.

GRAND UNION CANAL
- LEICESTER
NAVIGATION
- 3 1/2 MILES

- allow 1 1/4 hours.

•• •• •• *- B675 - Barrow Upon Soar - Grand Union Canal - Pilling's Lock - Woodthorpe Bridge - Meadow Farm - B675 - Barrow Upon Soar.*

- 1:25,000 Pathfinder Series Sheet No. 874 (SK41/51) Loughborough (South).

- No official one. Limited roadside parking on B675 at Grid Ref. SK573174.

- Close to the start are - The Riverside Inn and Soar Bridge Inn.

ABOUT THE WALK - A delightful walk along part of the Leicester Navigation section of the Grand Union Canal. You start overlooking the Barrow Lock, and head northwards along the towpath to Pilling Lock, where the canal returns briefly to the River Soar. You cross over to the otherside of the canal and continue to Woodthorpe Bridge. From here you cross fields back to Barrow-upon-Soar. You can always walk back along the canal and explore more of the Barrow lock area, both of which are highly recommended.

WALKING INSTRUCTIONS - From the B675 bridge over the River Soar, close to the inns -Riverside and Soar Bridge, leave by the western (Quorn) side and head northwards along the well defined path. On your right is the River Soar, which you walk beside for 3/4 mile to Pilling Lock. Here the river and its weir is avoided by the Leicester Navigation of the Grand Union Canal. Cross the footbridge over the canal and continue along the righthand side. In a 1/3 mile pass Top Bridge and in little more than a 1/4 mile later gain Woodthorpe Bridge. Here leave the canal and cross the bridge, and continue along the field edge on a defined track. Pass woodland on your left and 1/4 mile later leave the track via footbridge on your left. Keep a fence on your right with a lake beyond. Aim for the righthand end of a small wood, where there is a footbridge. Cross the field beyond to the far righthand corner to a stile. Bear right along the field edge to another stile and footbridge. Here

- Continued opposite -

RATBY AND THORNTON RESERVOIR - 9 MILES

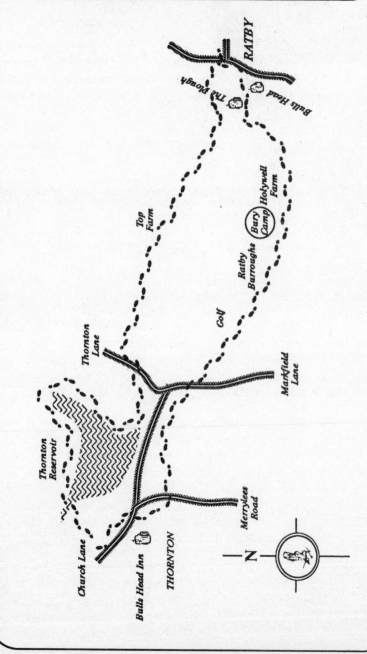

RATBY AND THORNTON RESERVOIR
- 9 MILES
- allow 3 1/2 hours.

Walk No
11

- *Ratby - Holy Well - Change Spinney - Crow Wood - Thornton - Thornton Reservoir - Top Farm - Ratby.*

O.S. MAP - *1:25,000 Pathfinder Series Sheet No. 894 (SK40/50) - Leicester (West) & Market Bosworth.*

- No official one. Walk starts from Ratby church where there is roadside parking. Car Park at Thornton Reservoir.

- The Plough and Bull's Head, Ratby. Bull's Head, Thornton.

ABOUT THE WALK - The longest in the book but an outstanding one! The walk across the fields and woodland to Thornton is exceptional and in April the woodland was carpeted with bluebells. Thornton Reservoir is beautifully located and can be walked around as a very pleasant 2 mile walk in its own right. You return over the fields, maintaining the walks high character, back to Ratby. I am very biased about this walk, but I did it in perfect weather - got sunburnt! - and was very impressed with this area.

WALKING INSTRUCTIONS - Descend Church Lane to the main road in Ratby and turn left. Pass the library and just afterwards turn right along Burroughs Road, with the Bull's Head on your left. A little way along the lane on your right is The Plough Inn. Continue a few yards more to a stile on your left. At the end of the field turn right over the stile, Cross two more stiles before bearing left to another and a footbridge beyond. Turn right now on a track and keep the stream on your right for more than 1/2 mile. Pass the turn off for Holywell Farm and continue near the stream to two gates. Continue to another on the edge of Change Spinney; far to your right is earthworks of Bury Camp. Continue beside woodland then through it to a gate. Continue ahead to another and keep straight ahead on a wide track - a bridleway - lined by woodland. After 1/4 mile pass a golf course on your left. Keep on this track for 3/4 mile to a minor road on the right of Polebrook Wood.

Go straight across to a stile and path sign. The path is not defined but keeps to the field edge, with the road over the hedge, to a stile. You continue beside the field hedge to another stile before descending to a footbridge on the lefthand side of the water works associated with Thornton Reservoir. The reservoir comes into view as you descend. Continue to another stile and ascend the field to a stile and road - Merrylees Road - opposite a petrol station. Turn right and at the road junction left along Main Street of Thornton passing the Bull's Head Inn. Shortly afterwards turn right down Church Lane and pass Thornton church and continue descending on a path to the track around Thornton Reservoir. Turn left and walk around the reservoir - about 1 1/2 miles - to the minor road.

Turn left along the road for a few yards to a stile and footpath sign on your left. Ascend the field to a stile in the top lefthand corner. Continue along the next field with the hedge on your left to a stile and footpath sign and road - Thornton Lane. Turn left and in 50 yards right at the stile and footpath sign. Walk along the field edge to a gate and cross the next field to a stile in the far righthand corner. The path is now a fenced one as you approach Top Farm. Walk around the righthand side of it and gain the track/drive and follow it to a lefthand corner. Here turn right along the field edge to a stile on your left in a few yards. Turn left and keep to the field edge for two fields before swinging right to a track. Follow this for 150 yards to a stile. Keep a stream on your left then right and cross two footbridges before reaching a lane you walked along at the start. You can follow this past The Plough Inn and retrace your steps back to Ratby church. Or turn left through a stile on your left, after a few yards, and diagonally cross the field to a stile. Cross the next field for a short distance before turning left inbetween the houses into Stamford Street. Turn right and descend to the main road and turn left then right into Church Lane where you began.

Thornton Reservoir - western end.

Thornton and Thornton Reservoir.

Pilling's Lock - see walk 10.

DONINGTON LE HEATH & SNIBSTON CHAPEL - 3 MILES

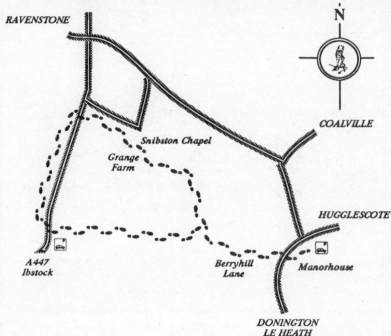

RAVENSTONE

N

COALVILLE

Snibston Chapel

Grange Farm

HUGGLESCOTE

A447 Ibstock

Berryhill Lane

Manorhouse

DONINGTON LE HEATH

DONINGTON LE HEATH MANOR HOUSE - dates from the 14th century. Has been restored and furnished with 16th and 17th century oak furniture. Beside the car park is an Iron Age settlement.

DONINGTON LE HEATH AND SNIBSTON CHAPEL - 3 MILES

- allow 1 1/4 hours.

•• •• •• *- Donington Le Heath Manor House - Snibston church - Ravenstone - Kelham Bridge Farm - Donington Le Heath.*

- 1:25,000 Pathfinder Series Sheet No. 874 (SK 41/51) - Loughborough (South).

Donington Le Heath Manor House. Beside A447 near Kelham Bridge Farm, Grid Ref. 4051213.

- None on the route, but several in Coalville. Tea room at the Manor House.

ABOUT THE WALK - A short walk starting from the beautifully preserved Manor House - well worth visiting. You cross the fields to the remote Snibston chapel dedicated to St. Mary, dating back to 1150 A.D. A short road walk brings you to a path over the field back to Donington Le Heath.

WALKING INSTRUCTIONS - Walk through the grounds of the Manor House and visit the house. Reaching the road turn right then left along Berryhill Lane - you return along the lane at the end. Approaching the first houses on your right, turn right and follow the well defined path along the field edge to a stile. Over this bear left and descend slightly to another stile. Continue on a track to Grange Farm and Snibston chapel on your left. Continue ahead on the lane to Ravenstone and the A447 road, little over 1/4 mile away. Turn left along the A447 and walk beside it for little over 1/2 mile - there is a wide grass verge and path. Pass Coalfield North Open cast on your right. Soon afterwards on your left is a stile and footpath sign, just before the car park. Turn left over the stile and left to another before descending to a footbridge. The area has one of the biggest nettle beds I have ever seen! Cross the footbridge and begin ascending on the distinct path which later becomes a lane as you re-enter Berryhill Lane. Retrace your steps back to the Manor House and car park - perhaps the tea room?

MOIRA AND
THE ASHBY CANAL - 1 MILE

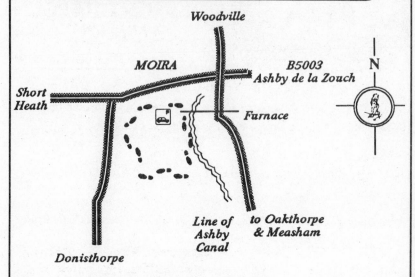

Woodville

MOIRA

B5003
Ashby de la Zouch

Short
Heath

N

Furnace

Line of
Ashby
Canal

to Oakthorpe
& Measham

Donisthorpe

MOIRA FURNACE -
Dates from the early 19th
century and is "The best
preserved example of a
coke fuelled iron-smelt
furnace in Britain." The
furnace museum is open
in the afternoon each
weekend from Easter to
October. Adjacent are craft
workshops.

MOIRA AND THE ASHBY CANAL - 1 MILE

- allow 1/2 hour.

•• •• •• - *Moira Furnace - Line of Ashby Canal - Moira.*

- *1:25,000 Pathfinder Series Sheet No. 873 (SK 21/31) - Ashby de la Zouch.*

- *Moira Furnace/ Grid Ref. SK 315152.*

- *None!*

ABOUT THE WALK - By far the shortest in the book!. Two other walks explore the navigatable section of the Ashby Canal but I include this walk to show you its northern end - the abandoned section. In its hey day it was very active serving the surrounding coal mines, but the canal demise is largely attributable to the fact that it was not a through route. Had the canal been extended to the Trent & Mersey Canal as envisaged it would have become a major link in the canal network. Alas this was not to be. At Moira you can walk along the filled line of the canal and see the most impressive furnace. The walk can be extended to follow the 2 1/4 mile Moira Trail.

WALKING INSTRUCTIONS - From the car park walk to the furnace and abandoned canal. Turn right along the path, following the line of the canal for less than 1/4 mile. Turn at a stile and cross to another and a track. Follow this a short distance to the railway and turn right along the road past the houses. Where it turns left under the railway keep ahead on a track, guided by yellow posts. After a few yards turn right and cross the playing field area- Crescent Park - to the Furnace Road and turn right back to the car park and furnace.

ASHBY CANAL - 22 miles long without a lock and dates from 1794. Originally extending from Marston Junction to Moira, but the section from near Snarestone Tunnel to Moira is abandoned and mostly filled in.

SHACKERSTONE & THE ASHBY DE LA ZOUCH CANAL - 5 1/2 MILES

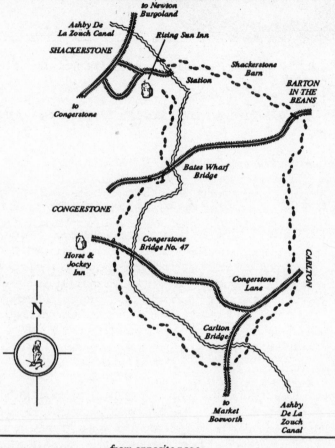

- from opposite page -

Turn right along the "Main Street" of Carlton. Walk past Bank Farm on your left and continue on the lane - Congerstone Lane. Pass under the railway line and bear left to Carlton Bridge No.44. Here descend to the Ashby canal and walk along the towpath with the canal on your righthand side. In 1/4 mile pass the canal milestone - 16/14 miles. Keep on the canal towpath for the next 2 miles back to Shackerstone. After a mile pass under Congerstone Bridge No. 47 - the Horse & Jockey Inn is "100 yards" away! Continue to Turn Bridge No. 52 at Shackerstone and gain the road. Turn left back into the village where you began.

SHACKERSTONE & THE ASHBY DE LA ZOUCH CANAL
- 5 1/2 MILES
- allow 2 hours.

•● ●● ●● *- Shackerstone - Barton in the Beans - Carlton - Carlton Bridge - Ashby de la Zouch Canal - Shackerstone.*

- 1:25,000 Pathfinder Series Sheet No. 893 (SK20/30) - Tamworth.

- No official one.

- Rising Sun Inn, Shackerstone; Horse & Jockey Inn, Congerstone - "100 yards from route." Tearooms at Shackerstone Station and in Barton in the Beans. At Newton Burgoland 1 1/2 miles north of Shackerstone is the Belper Arms - the oldest inn in Leicestershire dating back to 1290 A.D.

ABOUT THE WALK - Shackerstone is a very attractive village beside the Ashby canal. First you follow a track across the fields to Barton in the Beans before heading south to the village of Carlton. As I crossed these fields I heard my first cuckoo of the year. Beyond Carlton you gain the Ashby canal and follow it for more than two miles back to Shackerstone. The canal is particularly attractive and no doubt a narrow boat will be seen as you walk the towpath.

WALKING INSTRUCTIONS - Starting from the church in Shackerstone walk along Church Street past the Rising Sun Inn and turn right along Station Road. In a few yards cross Turn Bridge No. 52 on the Ashby canal - you return to here at the end of the walk. To your right is the road to Shackerstone Station. Continue on the road and pass under the railway line and soon follow a concrete farm road to Shackerstone Barn. Go through a gate and keep straight ahead with a fence on your left to another gate and footpath sign. Continue ahead soon walking along a track which leads you into the village of Barton in the Beans. Joining the Main Street follow it for a few yards before turning right, as footpath signed - "Carlton". Walk through the farm and follow the well marked path with yellow topped posts. Cross four fields to a track. Turn right then left and keep the hedge on your left and reach a stile. Cross the next field to a stile and the following one, aiming for the righthand side of the church dedicated to St. Andrew.

- continued opposite -

MARKET BOSWORTH, BATTLE OF BOSWORTH & ASHBY CANAL
- 8 1/2 MILES

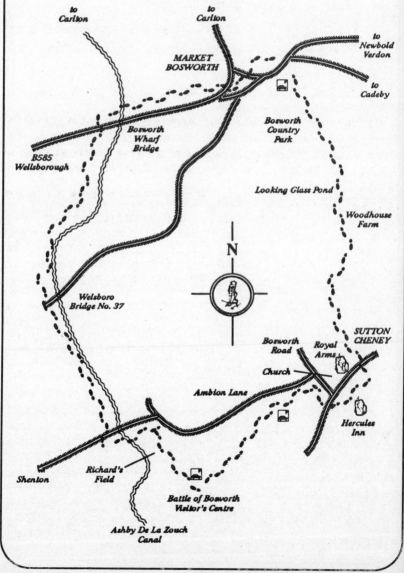

to Carlton

to Carlton

MARKET BOSWORTH

to Newbold Verdon

to Cadeby

Bosworth Wharf Bridge

B585 Wellsborough

Bosworth Country Park

Looking Glass Pond

Woodhouse Farm

N

Welsboro Bridge No. 37

SUTTON CHENEY

Bosworth Road

Royal Arms

Church

Ambion Lane

Hercules Inn

Shenton

Richard's Field

Battle of Bosworth Visitor's Centre

Ashby De La Zouch Canal

MARKET BOSWORTH, BATTLE OF BOSWORTH & ASHBY CANAL - 8 1/2 MILES

- allow 3 1/2 hours.

•• •• •• *- Market Bosworth - Bosworth Country Park - Sutton Cheney - Battle of Bosworth Country Park - Ashby de la Zouch Canal - Market Bosworth.*

- 1:25,000 Pathfinder Series Sheet No. 894 (SK 40/50) - Leicester (West) & Market Bosworth.
- 1:25,000 Pathfinder Series Sheet No.893 (SK 20/30) - Tamworth.

- Bosworth Country Park, beside the B585 road. Grid Ref. 412032.

- several in Market Bosworth. Royal Arms and Hercules Inn, Sutton Cheney.

ABOUT THE WALK - Quite simply - outstanding! First you walk through Bosworth Park along a stunning avenue of trees before reaching the historically interesting village of Sutton Cheney. Here a visit to the church, dedicated to St. James, is a must - King Richard 111 heard mass here on August 22nd 1485 before the Battle of Bosworth. Leaving the village you head for Ambion Hill and the Battle of Bosworth Country Park. The path leads you through the battle ground with plaques detailing the various stages of the battle. You descend to Richard's Field where King Richard 111 died, before gaining the Ashby canal. 2 miles of peaceful walking along here, gives you time to reflect on the events five centuries ago, before leaving the canal and walking along the road into Market Bosworth and back to the car park.

WALKING INSTRUCTIONS - From the car park cross the open meadow to your right, aiming for the righthand side of the pond. Keep to the paths beneath the pond, walking through the arboretum. Beyond the pond and on the edge of the woodland you will find a small gate. Go through this and follow a well defined track along an avenue of trees. After less than 1/2 mile pass Looking Glass Pond on your right. Soon afterwards pass Woodhouse Farm on your left and continue descending on the track and cross a stream.

Ascend the other side and bear right on the defined path/track across a field. Reaching the field edge turn right on the track with the hedge on your left. Part way through this field turn left and walk through the Royal Arms to the road! Turn right into Sutton Cheney passing Hall Farm on your left and the Hercules Inn. Just after turn right into the churchyard of St. James church and visit the church. Exit the otherside onto Bosworth Road.

Turn right then left along Ambion Lane and in 1/4 mile gain Cheney Lane car park. Walk through the car park to the gate and footpath and follow it to the Battlefield Centre of the Battle of Bosworth Country Park. You will more than likely see various standards flying ahead, indicating the location of the various armies in the battle. Walk past the Battlefield Centre on your left and across the car park to the footpath/battle trail on your right. The path leads over Ambion Hill and down to railway line and Station Farm. As you follow the path you are following the battle trail and at key locations a plaque details that part of the battle. At the road by Station Farm turn right and you soon reach Richard's Field on your left. After visiting the site return to the road and continue along it and turn left to pass under an aqueduct of the Ashby de la Zouch canal. Turn left and ascend to the canal towpath and cross the aqueduct and follow the towpath with the canal on your right, for the next 2 miles. Soon pass milepost 13/17 and 14/16 before passing under bridges 39 to 41. Gaining Bridge No. 42 - Bosworth Wharf Bridge ascend to the road - B585 - and turn right and walk into Market Bosworth 3/4 mile away. Reaching the centre turn right then left keeping on B585 to reach the car park where you began at Bosworth Country Park.

SUTTON CHENEY - The church dedicated to St. James dates back to the 13th century. Here on August 22nd 1485 King Richard 111 heard mass for the last time, before the battle. Inside are several memorials; one large one to Sir William Roberts, who died in 1633. He built the impressive Almshouses on the right of the church. A modern memorial erected by the Society of Richard 111 is the centre piece of an annual Richard 111 Memorial Service, held on the nearest Sunday to August 22nd.

THE BATTLE OF BOSWORTH - Ended the War of the Roses on August 22nd 1485, when King Richard 111 was killed and Henry Tudor became king. Going into battle King Richard exclaimed - "I live a king; if I die, I die a king."

Former Almshouses, Sutton Cheney.

Richard's Field.

WALK RECORD CHART

Date walked.

1.BREEDON ON THE HILL - 2 MILES ....

2.ASHBY DE LA ZOUCH - 5 MILES...

3.OSGATHORPE & GRACE DIEU PRIORY - 5 MILES...........................

4.MOUNT ST. BERNARD ABBEY & BLACKBROOK RESERVOIR -
5 MILES..

5.BEACON HILL - 2 MILES ....

6.ULVERSCROFT PRIORY - 4 1/2 MILES...

7.BARDON HILL & WARREN HILLS - 5 1/2 MILES.............................

8.SWITHLAND WOOD - 2 1/2 MILES ....

9.BRADGATE PARK - 4 MILES...

10.GRAND UNION CANAL - LEICESTER NAVIGATION - 3 1/2
MILES..

11.RATBY AND THORNTON RESERVOIR - 9 MILES...........................

12.DONINGTON LE HEATH & SNIBSTON CHAPEL - 3
MILES..

13.MOIRA AND THE ASHBY CANAL - 1 MILE ....

14.SHACKERSTONE & THE ASHBY DE LA ZOUCH CANAL - 5 1/2
MILES..

15.MARKET BOSWORTH, BATTLE OF BOSWORTH & ASHBY
CANAL - 8 1/2 MILES...

THE JOHN MERRILL WALK BADGE

Complete six of the walks in this book and get the above special badge and signed certificate. Badges are black cloth with lettering and walking man embroidered in four colours and measure 3 1/2" in diameter.

(BADGE ORDER FORM)

Date walk completed...

....

NAME ....

ADDRESS ....

....

Price: £3.00 each including postage, VAT and signed completion certificate.
Amount enclosed (Payable to El Morro Equipment Ltd) ..

From: **El Morro Equipment Ltd.,**
Milne House, Speedwell Mill, Millers Green,
Wirksworth,, Derbyshire. DE4 4BL.

✆ /**Fax** (01629) 826354 - 24hr answering service.

********** *YOU MAY PHOTOCOPY THIS FORM* ***********

"I'VE DONE A JOHN MERRILL WALK" T SHIRT -

Emerald Green with white lettering and walking man logo. Send £7.50 to El Morro Equipment Ltd., stating size required.

John Merrill's "Happy Walking!" Cap - £3.00

JOHN MERRILL'S CHARNWOOD FOREST CHALLENGE WALK

Now you have walked to all of the major places of Charnwood Forest, individually, now walk them all in a day by following John Merrill's

"Charnwood Forest Challenge Walk"

- 25 miles and 2,500 feet of ascent.

The successful can apply for a special four colour embroidered badge and signed certificate!

ootprint
Award

OTHER CHALLENGE WALKS
BY JOHN N. MERRILL

DAY CHALLENGES -

John Merrill's White Peak Challenge Walk - 25 miles.
Circular walk from Bakewell involving 3,600 feet of ascent.

John Merrill's Dark Peak Challenge Walk - 24 miles.
Circular walk from Hathersage involving 3,300 feet of ascent.

**John Merrill's Staffordshire Moorlands Challenge Walk
- 26 miles.** Circular walk from Oakamoor involving 2,200 feet of ascent.

John Merrill's Yorkshire Dales Challenge Walk - 23 miles.
Circular walk from Kettlewell involving 3,600 feet of ascent.

John Merrill's North Yorkshire Moors Challenge Walk - 24 miles.
Circular walk from Goathland - a seaside bash - involving 2,000 feet of ascent.

The Little John Challenge Walk - 28 miles.
Circular walk from Edwinstowe in Sherwood Forest - Robin Hood country.

Peak District End to End Walks.
1. Gritstone Edge Walk - 23 miles down the eastern edge system.
2. Limestone Dale Walk - 24 miles down the limestone dales from Buxton to Ashbourne.

The Rutland Water Challenge walk - 24 miles
Around the shore of Rutland Water, the largest man made reservoir in Britain.

The Malvern Hills Challenge Walk - 20 miles.
Beneath and along the crest of the Malvern Hills.

The Salter's Way - 25 miles.
Across Cheshire from Northwich to the Pennines, following an old salt way.

John Merrill's Snowdon Challenge Walk - 30 miles.
A tough day walk involving 5,000 feet of ascent and descent from the sea to the summit of Snowdon AND BACK!

John Merrill's Three Counties Challenge Walk - 28 miles.
A tough walk from Tittesworth Reservoir over the Roaches, Shutlingsloe, Shining Tor and Flash - in Staffordshire, Cheshire and Derbyshire.

John Merrill's Charnwood Forest Challenge Walk - 25 miles

The grandslam of this area of north Leicestershire, starting from Bradgate Park, taking in several hill's and monastic buildings, involving 1,600 feet of ascent and descent

NEW TITLES -

The Quantock's Way - 24 miles.
Belvoir Witches Challenge Walk - 25 miles
Carneddau Challenge - 20 miles and 4,750 feet of ascent.

MULTIPLE DAY CHALLENGE WALKS -

The Limey Way - 40 miles

Down twenty limestone dales from Castleton to Thorpe in the Peak District in eight stages, starting and ending at Ashbourne. The finest longest distance walk in the Peak! Taking in the grandest and highest sights.

The River's Way - 43 miles.

Down the five main river systems of the Peak District, from Edale, the end of the Pennine Way, to Ilam.

The Peakland Way - 96 miles.

John Merrill's classic walk around the Peak District National Park, starting and finishing at Ashbourne. The route of eight stages takes in the variety of the Park - limestone dales, gritstone moorland, gritstone edges , historic buildings and trails. A route combing the finest assets the Peak District has. More than 7,000 people have walked the entire route since it was inugurated in 1974.

Peak District High Level Route - 90 miles

Clrcular walk from Matlock taking in the highest and remotest parts of the Peak District.

COASTAL WALKS & NATIONAL TRAILS -

The Cleveland Way - 112 miles around the North Yorkshire Moors and coast
- a truly exceptional walk.

The Isle of Wight Coast Path - 77 miles.

Complete encirclement of a magnificent island.

Walking Angelsey's coastline. - 130 miles.

- complete walk around a stunning coastline.

Forthcoming titles -

The Pembrokeshire Coast Path.	The Pilgrim's Way
The Ridgeway	The North Downs Way
Offa's Dyke Path	The South Downs Way

Snibston Capel - see walk 12.

Warren Hills - see walk 7.

REMEMBER AND OBSERVE THE COUNTRY CODE

Enjoy the countryside and respect its life and work.

 Guard against all risk of fire.

 Fasten all gates.

 Keep your dogs under close control.

 Keep to public paths across farmland.

 Use gates and stiles to cross fences, hedges and walls.

  Leave livestock, crops and machinery alone.

 Take your litter home - pack it in; pack it out.

 Help to keep all water clean.

 Protect wildlife, plants and trees.

Take special care on country roads

Make no unnecessary noise.

THE HIKER'S CODE

✿ Hike only along marked routes - do not leave the trail.

✿ Use stiles to climb fences; close gates.

✿ Camp only in designated campsites.

✿ Carry a light-weight stove.

✿ Leave the trail cleaner than you found it.

✿ Leave flowers and plants for others to enjoy.

✿ Keep dogs on a leash.

✿ Protect and do not disturb wildlife.

✿ Use the trail at your own risk.

✿ Leave only your thanks and footprints - take nothing but photographs.

EQUIPMENT NOTES
... some personal thoughts

BOOTS - *For summer use and day walking I wear lightweight boots. For high mountains and longer trips I prefer a good quality boot with a full leather upper, of medium weight, with a vibram sole. I always add a foam cushioned insole to help cushion the base of my feet.*

SOCKS - *I generally wear two thick pairs as this helps minimise blisters. The inner pair are of loop stitch variety and approximately 80% wool. - Thor-lo socks are excellent. The outer are a thick rib pair of approximately 80% wool.*

WATERPROOFS - *for general walking I wear a T shirt or cotton shirt with a cotton wind jacket on top. You generate heat as you walk and I prefer to layer my clothes to avoid getting too hot. Depending on the season will dictate how many layers you wear. In soft rain I just use my wind jacket for I know it quickly dries out. In heavy or consistant rain I slip on a neoprene lined cagoule, and although hot and clammy it does keep me reasonably dry. Only in extreme conditions will I don overtrousers, much preferring to get wet and feel comfortable. I never wear gaiters!*

FOOD - *as I walk I carry bars of chocolate, for they provide instant energy and are light to carry. In winter a flask of hot coffee is welcome. I never carry water and find no hardship from not doing so, but this is a personal matter! From experience I find the more I drink the more I want and sweat. You should always carry some extra food such as trail mix & candy bars etc., for emergencies.*

RUCKSACKS - *for day walking I use a climbing rucksack of about 40 litre capacity and although it leaves excess space it does mean that the sac is well padded, with an internal frame and padded shoulder straps. Inside apart from the basics for one day in winter I carry gloves, balaclava, spare pullover and a pair of socks.*

MAP & COMPASS - *when I am walking I always have the relevant map - preferably 1:25,000 scale - open in my hand. This enables me to constantly check that I am walking the right way. In case of bad weather I carry a compass, which once mastered gives you complete confidence in thick cloud or mist.*

"from footprint to finished book"

CIRCULAR WALK GUIDES -

SHORT CIRCULAR WALKS IN THE PEAK DISTRICT - Vol. 1 and 2
CIRCULAR WALKS IN WESTERN PEAKLAND
SHORT CIRCULAR WALKS IN THE STAFFORDSHIRE MOORLANDS
SHORT CIRCULAR WALKS - TOWNS & VILLAGES OF THE PEAK DISTRICT
SHORT CIRCULAR WALKS AROUND MATLOCK
SHORT CIRCULAR WALKS IN THE DUKERIES
SHORT CIRCULAR WALKS IN SOUTH YORKSHIRE
SHORT CIRCULAR WALKS IN SOUTH DERBYSHIRE
SHORT CIRCULAR WALKS AROUND BUXTON
SHORT CIRCULAR WALKS AROUND WIRKSWORTH
SHORT CIRCULAR WALKS IN THE HOPE VALLEY
40 SHORT CIRCULAR WALKS IN THE PEAK DISTRICT
CIRCULAR WALKS ON KINDER & BLEAKLOW
SHORT CIRCULAR WALKS IN SOUTH NOTTINGHAMSHIRE
SHIRT CIRCULAR WALKS IN CHESHIRE
SHORT CIRCULAR WALKS IN WEST YORKSHIRE
CIRCULAR WALKS TO PEAK DISTRICT AIRCRAFT WRECKS by John Mason
CIRCULAR WALKS IN THE DERBYSHIRE DALES
SHORT CIRCULAR WALKS IN EAST DEVON
SHORT CIRCULAR WALKS AROUND HARROGATE
SHORT CIRCULAR WALKS IN CHARNWOOD FOREST
SHORT CIRCULAR WALKS AROUND CHESTERFIELD
SHORT CIRCULAR WALKS IN THE YORKS DALES - Vol 1 - Southern area.
SHORT CIRCULAR WALKS IN THE AMBER VALLEY (Derbyshire)
SHORT CIRCULAR WALKS IN THE LAKE DISTRICT
SHORT CIRCULAR WALKS IN THE NORTH YORKSHIRE MOORS
SHORT CIRCULAR WALKS IN EAST STAFFORDSHIRE
DRIVING TO WALK - 16 Short Circular walks south of London by Dr. Simon Archer
LONG CIRCULAR WALKS IN THE PEAK DISTRICT - Vol.1, 2. and 3
LONG CIRCULAR WALKS IN THE STAFFORDSHIRE MOORLANDS
LONG CIRCULAR WALKS IN CHESHIRE
WALKING THE TISSINGTON TRAIL
WALKING THE HIGH PEAK TRAIL
WALKING THE MONSAL TRAIL & OTHER DERBYSHIRE TRAILS

CANAL WALKS -

VOL 1 - DERBYSHIRE & NOTTINGHAMSHIRE
VOL 2 - CHESHIRE & STAFFORDSHIRE
VOL 3 - STAFFORDSHIRE
VOL 4 - THE CHESHIRE RING
VOL 5 - LINCOLNSHIRE & NOTTINGHAMSHIRE
VOL 6 - SOUTH YORKSHIRE
VOL 7 - THE TRENT & MERSEY CANAL

JOHN MERRILL DAY CHALLENGE WALKS -

WHITE PEAK CHALLENGE WALK
DARK PEAK CHALLENGE WALK
PEAK DISTRICT END TO END WALKS
STAFFORDSHIRE MOORLANDS CHALLENGE WALK
THE LITTLE JOHN CHALLENGE WALK

YORKSHIRE DALES CHALLENGE WALK
NORTH YORKSHIRE MOORS CHALLENGE WALK
LAKELAND CHALLENGE WALK
THE RUTLAND WATER CHALLENGE WALK
MALVERN HILLS CHALLENGE WALK
THE SALTER'S WAY
THE SNOWDON CHALLENGE
CHARNWOOD FOREST CHALLENGE WALK
THREE COUNTIES CHALLENGE WALK (Peak District).
CAL-DER-WENT WALK by Geoffrey Carr,
THE QUANTOCK WAY
THE BELVOIR WITCHES CHALLENGE WALK.

<u>INSTRUCTION & RECORD</u> -
HIKE TO BE FIT.....STROLLING WITH JOHN
THE JOHN MERRILL WALK RECORD BOOK

<u>MULTIPLE DAY WALKS</u> -
THE RIVERS'S WAY
PEAK DISTRICT: HIGH LEVEL ROUTE
PEAK DISTRICT MARATHONS
THE LIMEY WAY
THE PEAKLAND WAY

<u>COAST WALKS & NATIONAL TRAILS</u> -
ISLE OF WIGHT COAST PATH
PEMBROKESHIRE COAST PATH
THE CLEVELAND WAY
WALKING ANGELSEY'S COASTLINE.

<u>CYCLING</u> *Compiled by Arnold Robinson.*
CYCLING AROUND THE NORTH YORK MOORS
CYCLING AROUND CASTLETON & the Hope Valley.

<u>PEAK DISTRICT HISTORICAL GUIDES</u> -
A to Z GUIDE OF THE PEAK DISTRICT
DERBYSHIRE INNS - an A to Z guide
HALLS AND CASTLES OF THE PEAK DISTRICT & DERBYSHIRE
TOURING THE PEAK DISTRICT & DERBYSHIRE BY CAR
DERBYSHIRE FOLKLORE
PUNISHMENT IN DERBYSHIRE
CUSTOMS OF THE PEAK DISTRICT & DERBYSHIRE
WINSTER - a souvenir guide
ARKWRIGHT OF CROMFORD
LEGENDS OF DERBYSHIRE
DERBYSHIRE FACTS & RECORDS
TALES FROM THE MINES by Geoffrey Carr
PEAK DISTRICT PLACE NAMES by Martin Spray
PEAK DISTRICT MONSTERS by Alan Smith

<u>JOHN MERRILL'S MAJOR WALKS</u> -
TURN RIGHT AT LAND'S END
WITH MUSTARD ON MY BACK
TURN RIGHT AT DEATH VALLEY
EMERALD COAST WALK

<u>SKETCH BOOKS</u> -
SKETCHES OF THE PEAK DISTRICT

<u>COLOUR BOOK:</u>-
THE PEAK DISTRICT.......something to remember her by.

<u>OVERSEAS GUIDES</u> -
HIKING IN NEW MEXICO - Vol I - The Sandia and Manzano Mountains.
Vol 2 - Hiking "Billy the Kid" Country. Vol 4 - N.W. area - " Hiking Indian Country."
"WALKING IN DRACULA COUNTRY" - Romania.

<u>VISITOR'S GUIDES</u> -
MATLOCK. BAKEWELL. ASHBOURNE.